NATIONAL GEOGRAPHIC

Vegetables

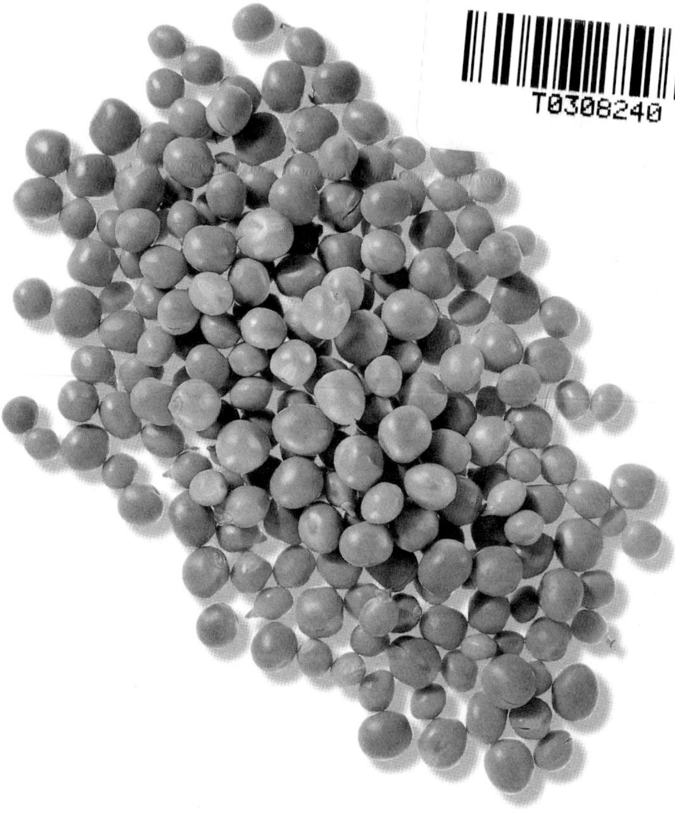

Dimi Stamos

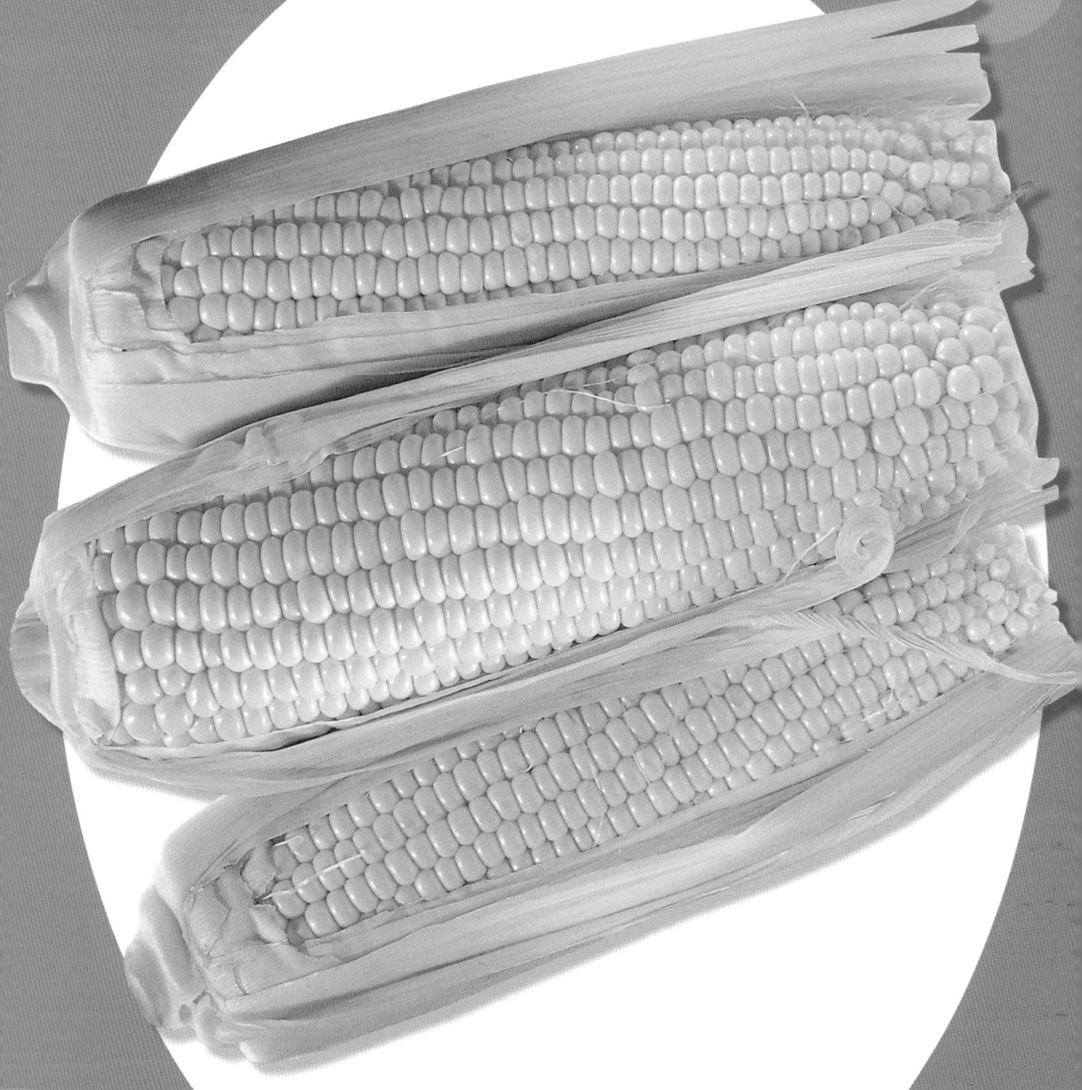

corn

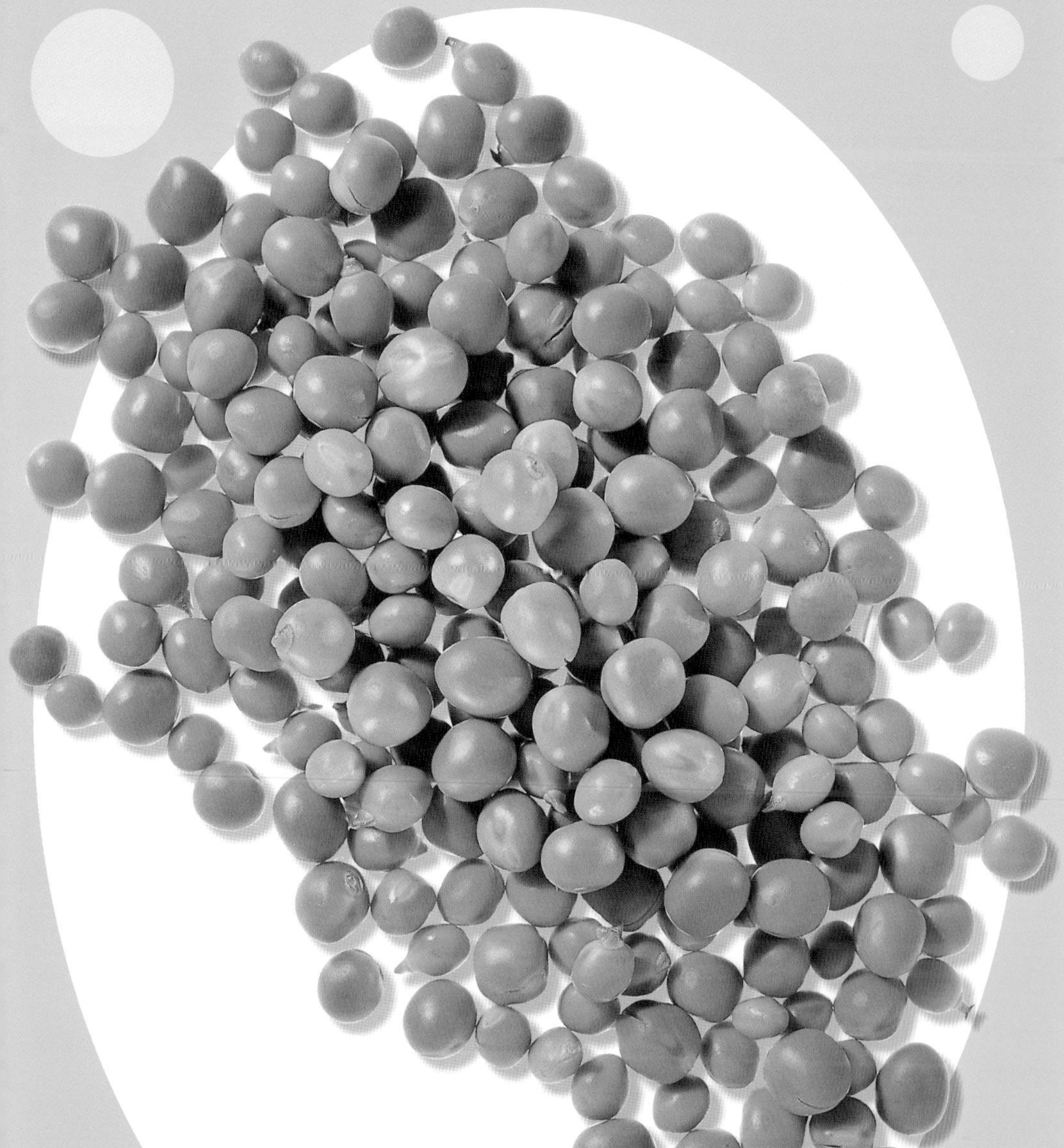

peas

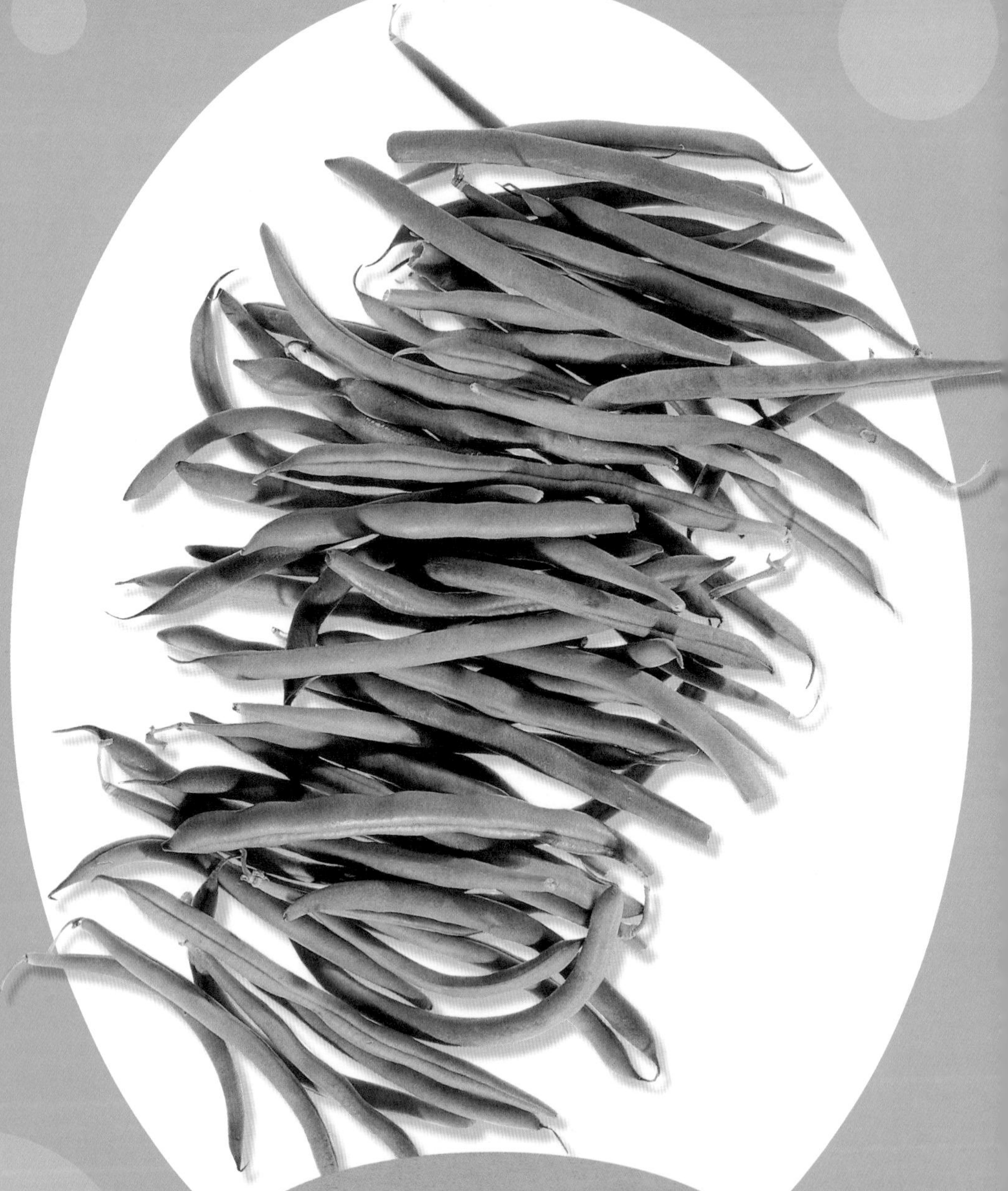

beans

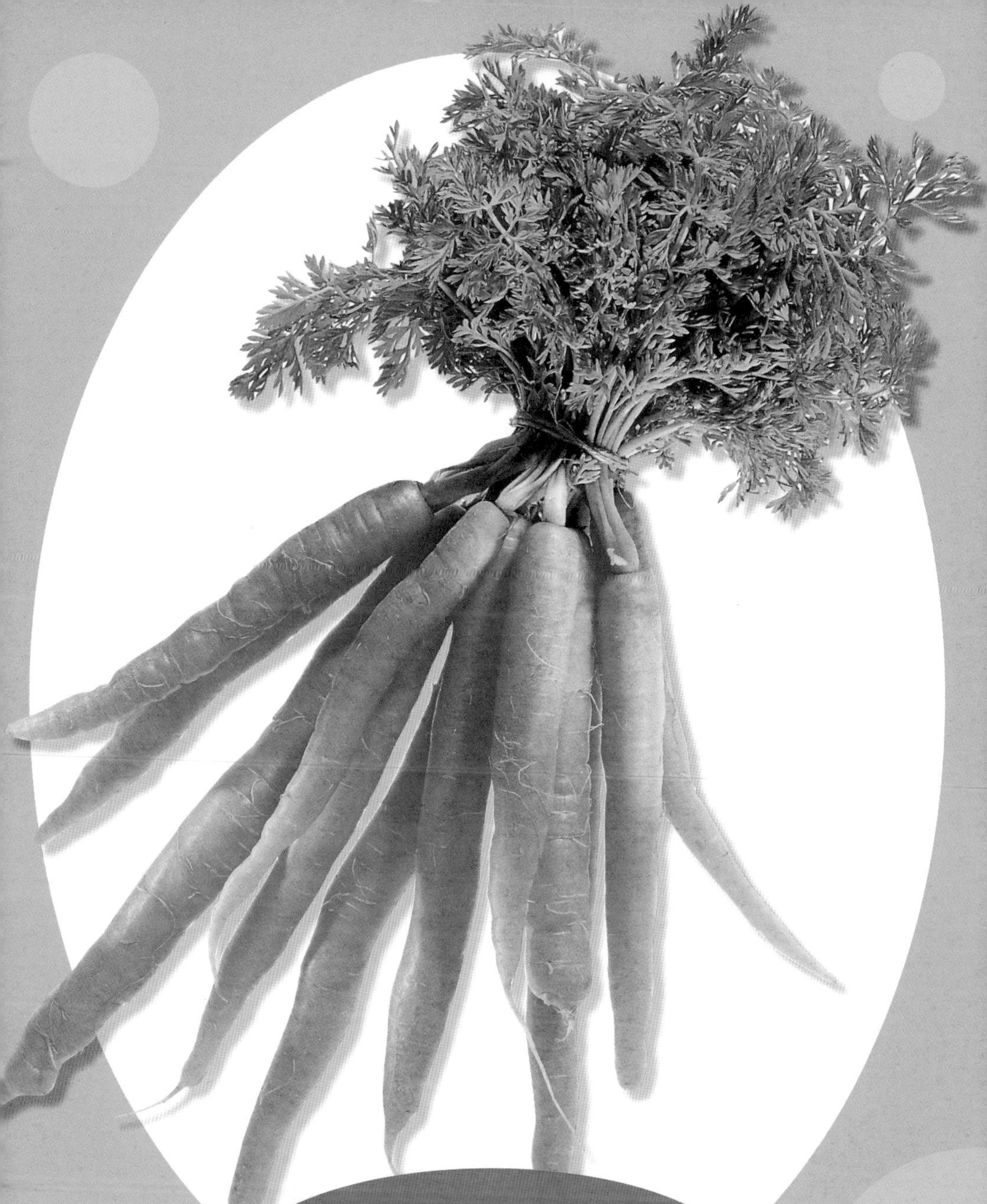

carrots

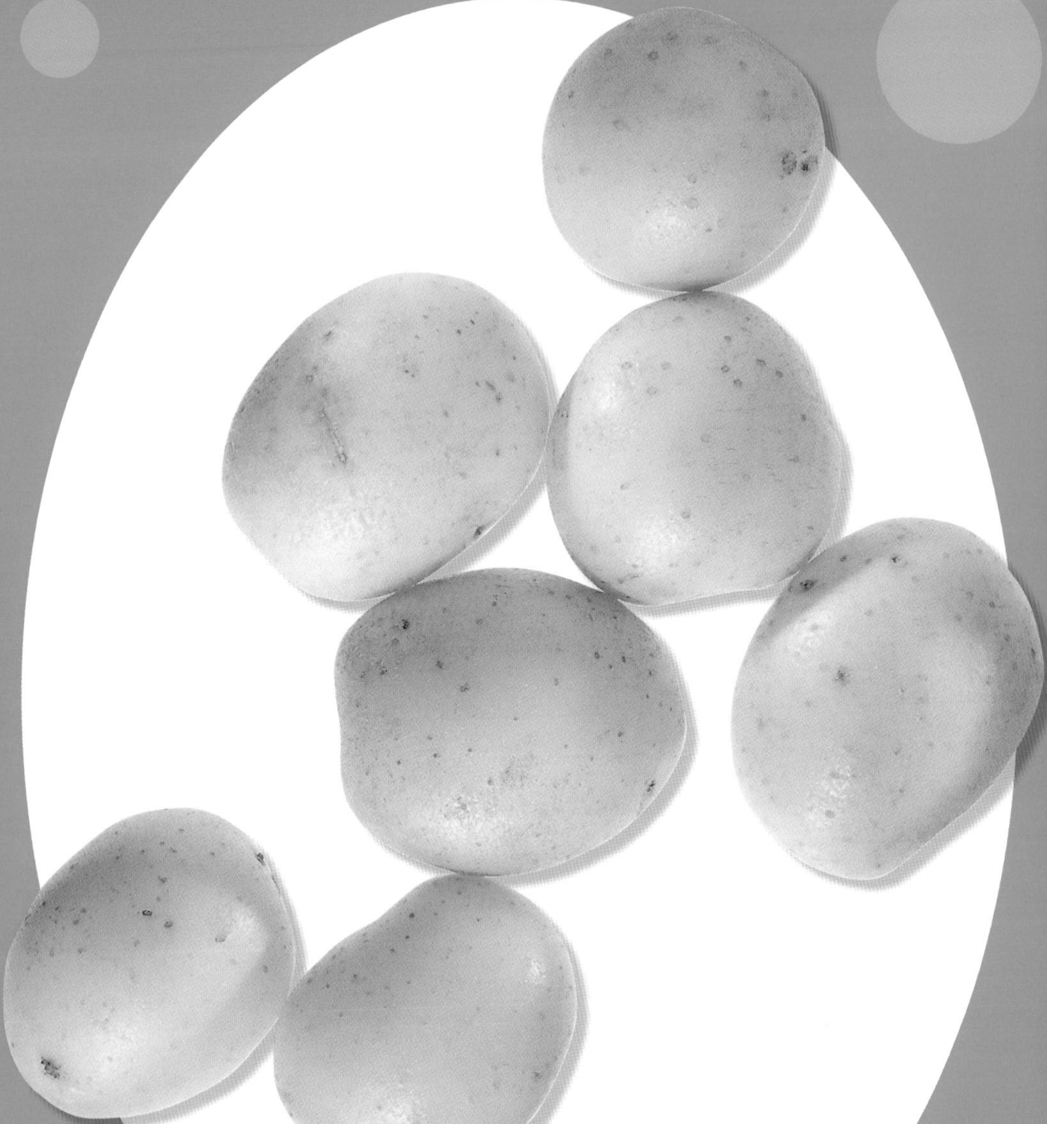

potatoes

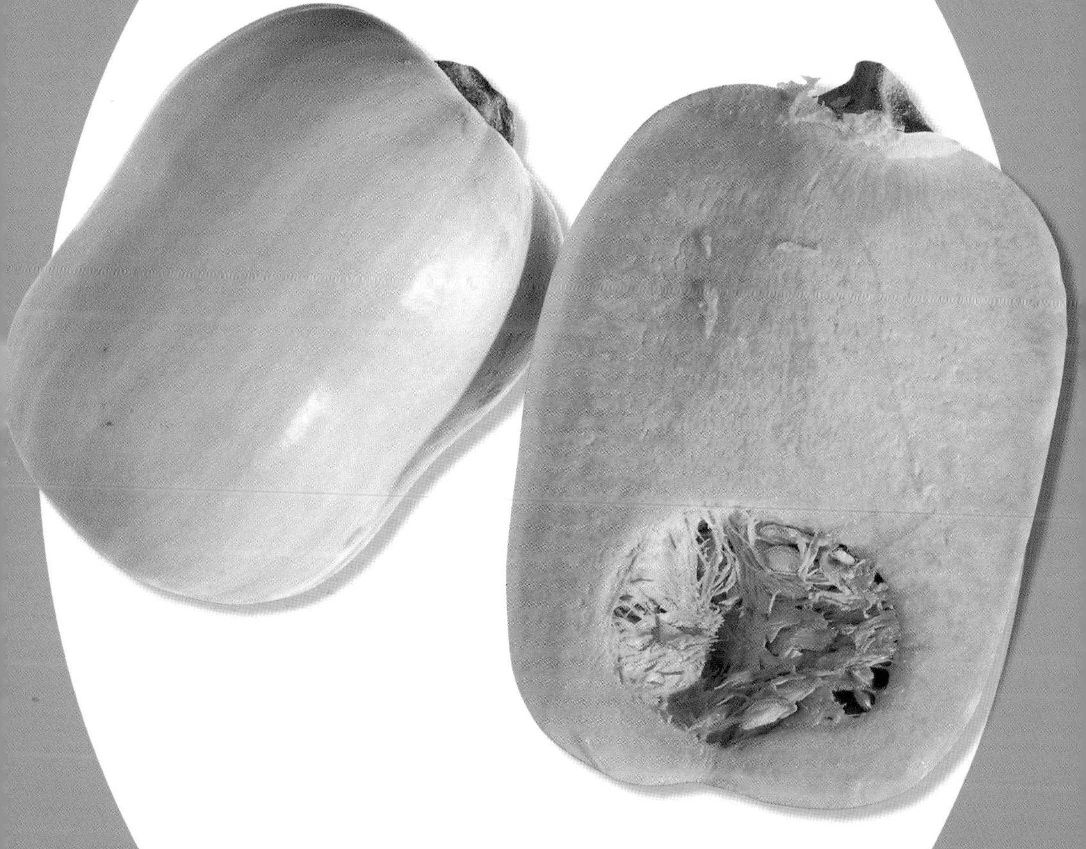

squash

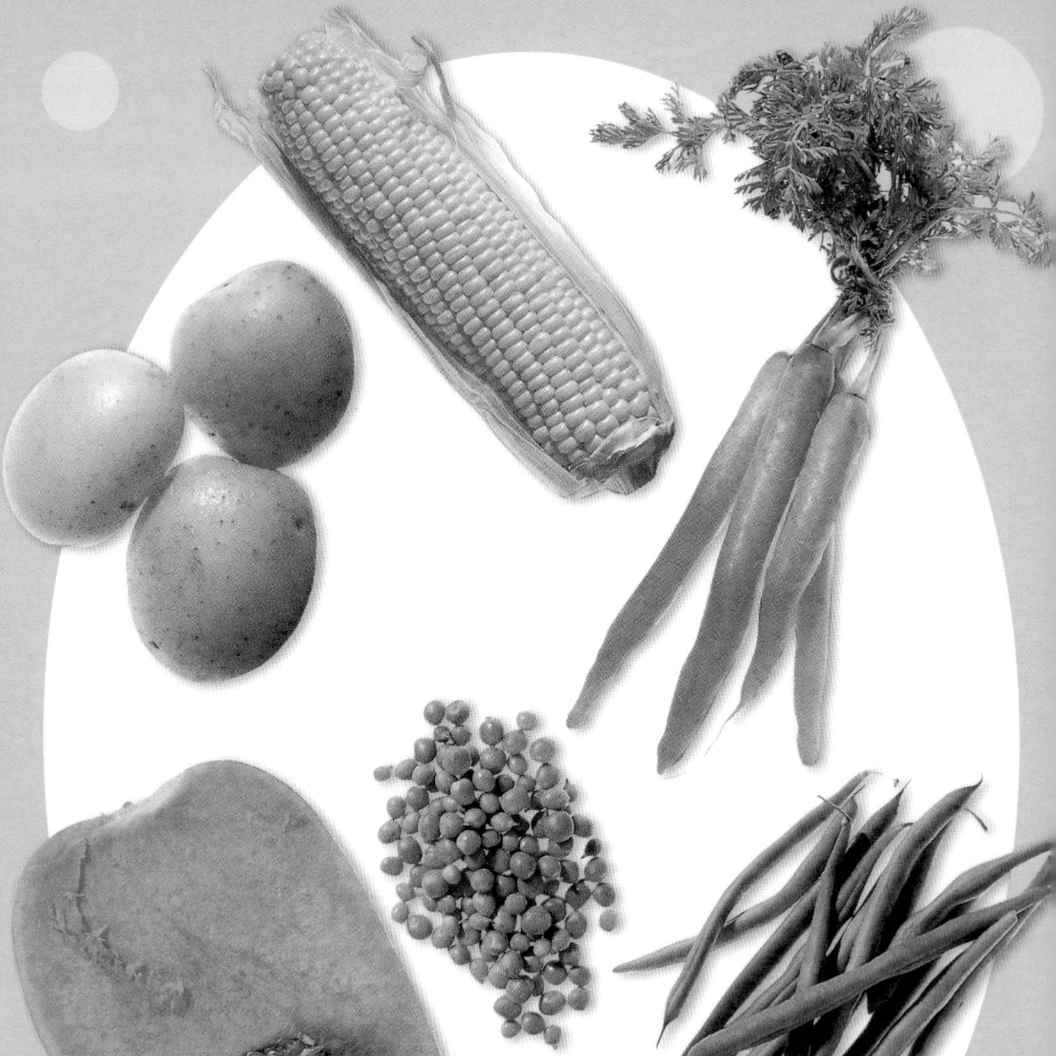

vegetables